Sanctified Memories

Jennie Clarke

Trafford rev. 07/16/2011

www.trafford.com
North America & international
toll-free: 1 888 232 4444 (USA & Canada)
phone: 250 383 6864 ♦ fax: 812 355 4082

Dedication

To my sons

and

their father

Acknowledgements

Piroska – Editor
Sister, Thank you for believing in me.

Joseph – Prologue
My dear friend, thank you for the guidance in my life.

Believe those who are seeking the truth.
Doubt those who find it.

~Andre Gide

Prologue

This collection is a poetic journey through the human condition. In these words, you will hear vivid portrayals of the human encounters with despair, grief, longing, lust, hope, love and divinity - a powerful journey through the levels of human consciousness. Let me present a viewpoint, which may signpost the divinity present underneath the words in this collection of art.

Time and time again in human history, it is out of the depth of the agony of despair that people have awakened up to the divinity, the depth of being, that was there all along. They have discovered that which makes the knowing and experience of life possible moment by moment. They have realized that they are not their emotions, their life histories, their memories, their beliefs, their bodies, but they are the one awareness in which these things take place.

This awareness is what all "others" are too underneath the diverse appearances. In this awareness, we move and have our being. The awareness of "everyone else" is as real as "mine" "You" and "me" can be regarded as different points of perception in one consciousness, one life, one being. We are all interconnected, all animated by one breath of life. This consciousness, this ultimate reality, is love without conditions. Totally affirming, totally accepting, and totally embracing.

The human mind can scarcely grasp the reality of divinity loving us not in spite of who we are, but exactly AS we are. We, humanity, are loved infinitely, perfectly, totally **WITH** all our pain, trauma and apparent mistakes. We are invited to quit judging ourselves, quit judging others, and accept this love - a love that loves us just as much whether we accept the invitation or not.

The more we recognize the unconditional love of divinity for ourselves, the more we can love others unconditionally. This is the basis of compassion. This poetry shines light into those aspects of ourselves we might rather avoid, it exposes the repressed nightmares we would prefer to forge. The more we bring the light of acceptance of all aspects of our psyche including the darker emotions – the more we can transcend them. Often we try to repress those parts of ourselves that we think are unlovable, yet nothing is unlovable in Reality.

Everything, which is illuminated by the light becomes part of the light. The human condition is part of Life, we are part of Life, and Life is the game of Divine Love, even if that love sometimes seems very deeply disguised. Very often, we find in life, that with hindsight difficult circumstances can be seen to have mysteriously worked out for good, that even hitting rock bottom was a necessary step in our evolution. Love was the highest intention behind all that we experienced whatever the intentions of the individual actors in the Play of Life.

Underneath all the happenings and drama of life, so vividly captured in this collection, everlasting unconditional love is our true nature. This is the mystic secret of the ages, this is the good news.

Love, peace, and blessings,

Joseph Cash
Author of *"This is The Dream"* and *"Beyond Identity"*

Memories to Illusions to Dreams

~ Brothers in Arms

Infinity in my hands of steel
reminds me to be gentle with my boys.

Skin of radiant pearls
carefully placed within my being.

In the womb, you encircled your bodies
through the tunnel of light
and not for a moment was there a chance
that you would not be mine in this life.

Little boys of bathing sands,
a grain with every smile.

It was you
that made this world complete,
I waited a long while.

In my arms you go to rest
closely against my heart.

In my dreams you stay with me,
gentle brothers to never part.

Through your souls so deeply divine
rests your father who seals the bind
of love that no one can take away
and I am grateful everyday.

~ For every moment, I stop to think

What language will my boys speak to me
when I have done my part.
The tools I gave,
the dreams we made
the laughter from our hearts.

Will distance follow them
when they leave this home?
Will they call to comfort me,
their mother, now old.

Wondering if, just if
did I do the right things?
Did I speak their native tongue?

All the moments that I keep.
Who will they love if not me?
And will they come back home?
Will the language change?
Will I feel estranged?
Someday I will know.

For every moment, I stop to listen
to the chatter and clatter of glee
will they recognize
that their mother cries
for she feels not worthy.

Where will I be when the moment arrives?
Will they stop in and say goodbye?
The answers remain a mystery to me,
and I cannot help to wonder in silence.

~ Aidan Glen

I will not contribute
to your loss
it only harbours
my own

I will not be selfish
to your tears
yet mine taste of Aidan
do yours?

I will not be resentful
to this god
for he does not decide
my right

I will tell you I miss my own
son this day
because I could not
give him life

I will set this grief free someday
when his wings are fully formed
and tell him that it was because of him
that his little brother was born.

I will see the shadows of his footprints
in the sidewalks next to mine
and hold his hand ever so tightly
as this death was so unkind.

~ Elizabeth

Elizabeth was your birth name

Angelica,
I gave to you
when you gave birth to me.

Your eyes so tender and lovely,
who took you to the stars?
Angelica darling, come home, you are so very far.

Pastures green and mountains high
Angelica went too soon when she died.
Who would have known it was to be
that I would love her endlessly.

Past the river and down the banks
through the town and off the planks,
beat the drums and play the horns,
for the body is gone, thus we mourn

Graced with beauty
oceans high
I missed to tell my longing's cry
when trees and branches swipe me by
I feel your spirit
and begin to cry.

~ Roach

Those mountains to dream of,

come now,

speak free again but leave all behind

dreams of children playing near the water brings freedom

mad prayer circles we form chanting

this, our soul's journeys

you wander quietly to your own place

sometimes, when it gets too crowded

it showers teardrops from God's lips

reminding you we are all going to be fine

water is salvation, a cleansing of spirits,

where lovers hand one another beautiful shells

each represents a listener in life

forever, a breeze of soft smiles

a splendor so tempting to bury for fear of loss

yet unnecessary because *joy* is now the only way

my prayer to you is to keep the fury of your essence

beyond reason should you reach now for love

taking the soothing of the summer winds

and storms to guide you

for

nothing and no one

should stop your spirit

from kind and giving love

picture those mountains like melting temples at your feet

a garden of prayer and Uriel, with you, kneeling,

the shapes and bumps no longer in your step

you deserve all the richness and wondrous glory

there is nothing in your shadow but a lighted stairway

so

tonight that cup of Divine wine that rests in front of you

carries

a toast to the magnificence of your new-found days

let no one come between your minds eye

~ Finding Ease

When my inner world collapses
I feel not awake from this night
yet the circumstances I so resist
make way to all things kind.

This notion of someone in pain,
the thought of someone in need,
in this world veiled by hurt
I want to just believe.

The ego has had a joyous ride on me
where it wishes to define
that the opponent is not my mind,
consciousness, there, my sign

Who is the last one standing in this mist
with strings tied to my wrists
I failed to take note and see
the ego trying to convince me

that love is not in my life
yet shelters were there when I cried
and only dreams were at my reach
ready, waiting, to welcome

me

~ Inter Be

Stillness soars to the top of the peak high
I embrace the quiet of the movement of the water
limitless space and distance
casts a brilliant cover around me

All have gone to sleep
the fish swaying in the clouds of seashore waves
the noise of the traffic over the distance hummed
the birds with rested chests from singing
the mind erases all activity entering only thoughts of *love*

God's presence radiates the deepest ocean

I am Higher
For I am with the Blessed One and He with me
I am the flower
to His soil
Transferring His love within me
To His love I am the spirit
To the spirit

We

Stillness reminds us of this

Stillness

is the dance of life where things were not as they seemed
the shadows we shed were not necessary
to protect what is not
illusions have no bearing on who we are

the people that are important hurt us with love
the observations made by others remain their filters
the honesty given with dignity

the courage to speak without wounding
the poise we leave where others have drawn swords
the responsibility of our families and friends
the falsehoods we never tell
the mantels of adornment that warm our hearts
and
no - box - can - compare
to *love*

no idol worshiping can bring me to a Higher purpose
only *love*

the wisest person seeks not a stage to speak
for, beyond words, images and fame
the individual rests

who knows *love* knows

One

Unity

is not preaching peace but practicing it
the conscious soul perceives a world held together

the broken living on the outskirts of the world
begging to be loved

yet

love does not assert itself in giving
it waits to be accepted
to be authentic is to

Simply Be

Tomorrow I shall rise
to a thousand more thoughts
but I can decide
which ones I shall take in
never to give power away
never to drain my spirit

again

For blessings are few but greater than most
and liberty of nothingness is a beautiful choice.

~ Conversations

You will never see me in the sunshine
how striking you are to me
how I love the sensation of
your demonstrative hands
my lips of temptress wine
the sound of your velvety clouded voice

illusions

I am worried
you will never know me
because we are two doomed ships
who have crossed lines
so many times
you move with haste
passing my vessel

memories

We are stuck in a space
where the windows are painted shut
and the smell of gasoline
has become normal and fragrant-like
we lapse in disguise
we move in marked territory
and live with average

dreams

Gifts

Love is always bestowed as a gift - freely, willingly and without expectation. We don't love to be loved; we love to love.

~Leo Buscaglia

~ To be the poem

tonight I lean my face against your cheek
we, poets, are more intimate in words
diction to the lover's *pocketbook*
a bulk of landscaped muse penning a paper
aching for someone to read them

You rest on my mind
ready for your translation of love
there have been moments my aura goes blind
that powerful sensation of you
between my thighs
vibrating

primavera

you, speechless, yet, pounding love

I am lost in your eyes

rumours chasing heads away from each other
delicious desires of you in my slumber
how does one recall the night spent in sex with poet
leaning bodies and striving thrusts

I do not want to be a phrase
in your pocketbook
of poetry
I want to be your poem

~ Shakespeare

I watched you sitting there
at the table with the checkerboard
mounted in the stone
your fingers beating against it
looking down at your pad
reading and rereading the things you
needed to tell her
your curly blonde hair, long, untidy and dirty
clothes stained and mouth dry
and I wondered who she was to put you,
lovely you,
in this state
not once did you look up
noticing only the words floating on the page
as the water streamed up closer
gentle waves teasing you to have a glance its way

I wanted to walk over to you but
who was I, like the ocean
unnoticed

you stopped beating,
writing now, flipping back, scratching your head
and brushing your sweaty brow
I watched and waited, hoping you would move away
from what ailed you, the pad, the page, a love
but you never moved

~ Milk

the box terrace home stinging for life
the smoky skies fill it
the northern side of who I am
and I watch from my window
never drawing the net curtains

I see him coming from Sunday to Thursday
5 am on the clock of my kitchen wall
he looks haggard, annoyed,
quiet
I want to love him
undress before him

the clatter of time moves forward
twisting us into forms of impatience
words have lived latent within us
I want to be his hearts desire
but the bottle is all he holds now

streets of cobblestones
the webs we lace to distance our feet
the pubs filled with young roses
he enters them on Friday night
I long for him to enter me

~ Sleep

my life has gone to sleep

but I still want to hear *"I love you"*

the cells under my skin flow even in death

If you want to know the woman

spread her legs with all your might

wide, as she may go,

for it is through the hole

often never told

the story of the woman

The hole –holier still

closed eyes never tell him

only hear her usual words

closed eyes never sing to him

only whine a maidens woes

closed eyes never escape with him

only trap her hole – whole

If you want to need her more

spread her thighs

look

deep

inside

it is there

no more to compare

the loss of a child

the scent of a cock

the taste of a tongue

the mourning, *take stock,*

When I told you, I needed you

you spread my legs

but

you closed your eyes

~ Gates

I want to know you

the you before you left

that tow-path we walked together

those blue trousers and that hat

fit tailor style

I want to remember you fussing

to open the cast ironed gate

looking around mortified with embarrassment

blushing

but you got it opened

the gate

leading

to

I want to see you again without fallen wing

before the plane

passed into the wrong direction

before you took the last breath

and entered the dawning sky

Perceptions

Jennie sees the damage in this world and clears it.
The wind

~ Joel Love

~ The Delivery

The delivery was present

Dubliners packed the streets to watch them arrive

Mammy going on baby 11

Would she really bring another home this time?

Crowds of drunkards hard at work

Stealing dole money off their wives

Whilst the sun dimmed over the road

To the house of many brothers mine

The main gate where the car was parked in

My grim faced father accompanied mushy heat

Mammy's grave overtones, half-eyed misery

What fools in rolling hills we must have appeared like?

Father only wanted things we simply were not

removed and calm

"a shag shouldn't always led to this messy lot!"

"Indeed my dear, but we are the Catholic"

~ In-difference

The toll is high against me

pressure of clots not flowing right

people wanting a piece of what is not theirs to have

inflictions of already scarred zones

I feel the indifference for those that talk

about things that need not be their business

but life is dreadful on their end

thus my world shows a better dialogue

and gossip IS the **devil's radio**

surrounded by the miscreant faces

"Did you know she so and so and so?"

Did you even ask me if I cared?

desensitize my mind when the preachers enter

the judges of this life are not one with mine

tune the radio to the left for damnation

or push the off button on their mouths

one -time

~ The Gossipers

It was rather revolting
That devil's radio – self-made, proclaimed,
retention and named
They talked about her
"er comes the ol mended whore"
GOSIPPERS
"She fucks em dark blokes ye know"
RIGHTEOUS
"a brood lot to feed after them nights of shagging"
UNAMUSED
Talk trickles over tea
Swollen hags wondering where their husbands are whilst
watching another virgin's hole leave for the night.
"She's looking for the meaty hand to pay for her cunt"
SHOCKING
"Oh Mary must we use such words!"
BLAME
"It's true you know, I heard from a lady at the grocers"
At least they were faithful
SMIRK
At least they stayed in and paddled their babies with a wooden
spoon to get them to bed early
Early enough to put on their self-made radio for the devils' talk
Why what else was there?
An eruption when their husbands came home
PISSED
At least talking about the fur-collared whore made them feel
important

INSIGHTFUL
generations of ideal chat
baby upon baby tuned in
everything seemed morbid as the kettle boiled
the bag was put in the pot
the cubes passed around
at least the ginger snaps weren't stale
Margaret always kept the front window clear and clean
the folded chairs unsnapped
to positioning their arses in line again
at least the virgin never disappointed – never once- to give these
women a bit of purpose
PERCEPTION
and just as their terrace stood symmetrical to the next
as did their bums
uniformly positioned chairs numbered
their husbands departing labour and
arriving home, had their tea, slept briefly then
gathered their hat and coat
LEFT
there was always a little peck for assurance
"I shan't be long love"
whilst down the dreadful road he trotted
 over the mud puddles in the rain

RADIO - TALK
the virgin always left shortly thereafter
in the same direction
but this was never given meaning
"what? – no – silly woman, she didn't go that way?"
Silently they sat, elbow to elbow
MORTIFIED
drowning into the faint light
Half one all gone
Half two all gone
Emptiness on the streets
HOME
Henry returned singing,
"Let me call you sweetheart I'm in"
"Shhhhhhh"
Margaret charged the stairs to help him in
up to bed
dragging his shoulders
heaving him up
It got cold during the night
Margaret reached for the window to shut it
as she reached to close the curtains
she looked down
there walked the whore
"I'm in love with youuuuuuu"
SILENT

So, the night fell on the village of twitching curtains

~ Amused

Perplexity amuses this ghost with the false faces I see.
Rich maniacal tramps that sit in waiting for the world to come
to their feet.

Judgment haunts their past as
they so beg condemnation onto me.
Weak words made to criticize my muse
feeds from corpses that bleed.

Gains in numbers and fake plastic hearts,
of posing to be righteous yet wrapped in their own lark.
Designing a life of mainstream gypsies with tattooed skin and
penniless wastebaskets of saving worthless pride are now
trashed in bins.

Gray, gloomy and cold against the cellars of eyes
Pretending to be gentle with Muse is *not* wise
Reinventing the pages and recreating the name
Yet soiling the friendships so anxiously gained

Older and lonely, uglier than spoiled wine,
a stench of false praying and the pot-smoking smiles.
Crouching down on twisted knees, a beseeching tone,
will never compare, pathetically, as you are left to moan.

~ Frank, the fucking poet

Kill Me ~ before you sleep

Love Me ~ before you weep

Eat Me ~ before your tea

Suck Me ~ before you bleed

Kiss Me ~ before you cum

Fuck Me ~ before you run

Frank was a fucking poet

who lived down the hall

collecting women like trophies

but none of them ever called

He saw my knickers hanging

in the warmth on a summer's day

I watched him watching them

Head trips blew him away

Frank was a filthy poet

who fell to his death

for nothing more than longing

to smell me wet

~ I cut into you

I cut into your hands
you who popped me
with your lucid tongue

I cut into your hands
you who wrote God's words
on the ends of my fingertips

I cut into your hands
you who broke my back
with gravity chasing pulls

those lamps, that light, the streets, the voices
the women who walk the night
from working for the men
carrying knives to protect themselves
from the hands that cut
following the brakes of the cars
that echo and honk for them
to come and cut into their hands

~ **My** drug lord

the laughter through my ghetto gate
the heroin drops on my silver plate
the leftovers of foes gone astray
and I am nothing without my fame

plastic people all around
the chemical smiles from their frowns
the drugs that keep us bent in shape
and I am everything for just one day

mediocre ain't where I am at
hustling the streets for my crack
the world my oyster in thick hands
and I am freedom in a zipper bag

you keep me steady in this artificial space
you are my friend without a face
the dreadlock lover that I chase
and I am dancing through your lace

the light that never seems to fade
my magic mushroom where I lay
through the fields of opium gaze
you drag my arms of needle track haze

~ Alpine

Down to her knickers she stood,
her breasts so weak, have despondingly died.

Perhaps this would convince him,
that he should find another female to lure,
another woman to press up against.

She passed through the stone street

"DO YOU SEE ME!"

Alpina shouted toward his skull

a quivering rock of shell
she lowered her body down,
with arms to her side

now removing the last bit of pride she had,
her knickers off, as she closed her eyes,

sedated, doped

he stood

Alpina turned to see,
if her body could resist,
any recourse from him.

What could he think of her being now,
but haggard, old and used,

a crowd dispersed as quickly as it formed
around her

Alpina positioned herself against his eyes,
now without closing them,
without looking away,
she shuddered the thought,
of him approaching her,
as he did just this,
closer and closer,
like venom vomited from a snake,
he drew nearer to her
until he was on top of her looking down.

"WHORE!"

~ Sacred Prostitute

a different bed

new pair of shimmering eyes

smell of ancient stench

a fucked up toilet

my glass is always unfilled

in the morning

no more which

colour makeup I have

he has disappeared

the least he could have said was

'need a ride?'

I stumble off the bed

made of coiled rubber sheets

now wet from last night's

forced lovemaking

the bathroom sink

looks the same as the last one

odious white bowls

no marks, no stories,

are comforted in my imagination

my shoes have been chewed at

that damned invisible dog

the window is mushroomed

it's hard to see the cars

passing to go to work

my day is done

love is an intersection

it never lasts an eternity

it comes with a price

each night

along with

an aching burn

~ Emotions

Intense emotions avoiding all just to be alone
Competing with the ego tis as she is known
The moments of discomfort rip through my bones
Facing yourself is necessary in order to grow
Urgent messages race straight to my soul
Aligning all perceptions about who I am
and what you aren't
Paradoxes are mirrors of blessing in disguise
If my words take over there will be no bias
I serve no purpose in this world completely
Worthy not are my actions without drawing in deeply
Affirming confidence and self assurance takes times
Renewing my faithful interventions for all things Divine

You can take me
make me
shake me
to whatever you please
control me
and
than scold me
but
never seize
to remember that I am human too,
and I bleed
I am tired of the shit you believe
so if you fuck with me
the walls will close in
and you will
feel
empty
again

~ Back

she wanted those things back

the things from the days when

his cotton t-shirt soaked in scented oils

off his skin that draped around her ribs

one raw fibre unprocessed

with chemicals from manufacturing companies

made in India where young children

are left for hours on a rug to pump out items

for sale on the backs of

fat-cats and cons

she wanted those days where he was her

poetry and she was his lavender bath

watching the candles lit dancing gently

to the healing music around them

and after this the tantric fest of sexual

orgasmic blows of ecstasy drug-infused nights

exploding through her veins and lashing out

an uncontrollable laughter releasing, hours later,

deafening tears of guilt and pain

she wanted the love that lived in her home to be

freed of the perceptions of curvier spines that tried to

rest on her back and blame her for love that did not

belong to them and she is now constantly reminded of

the knotting of serpents sliding around and her terror of

chopping their heads off

and what karmic inheritance this might bring,

so she holds back

but they keep coming and barking at her door,

angry that they did not get a chance inside,

the mind games of others who just did not understand

their life.

She wants those things
that took away her dignity
and spread pink liquid
through her chest cavity
of jealousy and ruin

to heave backwards into their manic hearts and

feed themselves of what she never hungered for.

She wants the life of sanity, of sleep, of contentment

but

it sits by her side pleading for her

to surrender

so that it might

be a tidal wave of acuity that she needs

as there is no awareness between free and will

without her acceptance that

what she wants and what she has is what she needs.

Always be ready to speak your mind
and the baseman will avoid you
~ William Blake

~ Forward to back

Flashbacks
come in forms of colours, and images
of nightmares never quite
dealt with
figures of mesh walls
lined with fake strength
and now
videos of trauma

re-the-experience

Exquisitely sensitive

my battling fatigue
stabbing my uneasy body
flash forward wishes
chest aching grief
and
I want nothing

but

truth

Physical

Now he has departed from this strange world a little
ahead of me.

~Albert Einstein

~ August (For Joseph)

There are moments when all the questions we want
answered in times of distress
are not present.

There are puzzle pieces lying against our feet that we
cannot reach immediately
and when we do they do not seem to fit.

There are visions of everlasting physical life, that when it is
taken so abruptly we are left hanging like an unfinished
painting that seems dull now.

Aren't paintings supposed to be beautiful?

When we approach all this there remains only one answer.

That is, that nothing truly matters but Love.

It is here,
it is in this energy
that is Love
that life and death are invisible
and
all that is
and
is of profound significance
is Love

as Love is Infinite and with love

one requires nothing more.

~ Luca

The day my brother died
I could hear the family breathing downstairs.
My upper bedroom carried vent sounds
of tears from my mother's heart.

Papa talked about the jar shut tight.
Canada placed him in it when he died.
There was nothing like this in the old country.
Mother wept with tormented eyes.

He was born still from waking.
The deaf tones of my mother's laborious pains;
petrified that she would lose him.
She passed out before he pushed through.

Today the walls close in when we enter the house.
A smell of bleach everywhere,
as if my mother longs to tidy
this reminiscence of coming home

bare

~ Apart from sin

I implore you
BE SILENT!
but I feel my heart heavy this eve
SILENCE!
I must explain to you sire that I don't want to die
BE GONE!
if I do not speak now I shall forever hold my peace
HOLD YOUR PEACE!
I am trying to survive
DEATH TO YOU!
I want to live
DIE!
I want not death, only life
NOW!
but why? why? morbid me, morbid cry
YOU WASTE MY TIME?
So I shall fade
TONIGHT!

As so the fairest maiden

REMOVE THE CANDLES
REMOVE HER LIGHT
REMOVE HER BODY
DRESSED IN WHITE
DRAW THE GARDEN
DRAW THE GROUND
DRAW HER BEAUTY
LAY HER DOWN

~ Follia

Death
you come to me
so sweet
with flight in your feet
and expect me to rush
without a word, a hush
and all I have had is heartache

yet speed fast you demand me
make
pressing on my cane
dancing against your orders
you came too soon

I never asked for this!

But Death what brings you to me
I am a mere man, a speck, a flea
dancing on the back of the meek
and you choose to take me?

Death, dear friend

unending - beast

Have you no pity?

~ Spit me dead

Oh 30 years

into this light

of crimson shades

of radiant nights

and of your mercy

I ask one thing

if you devour me

SUCK ME IN!

Through wasted tunnels

over channels of dune

into your soul

wicked spirits loom

find me torn

ripped to shreds

eat me whole

and spit me dead

~ Rocks

The night drew in, unforgiving and long
I sat in waiting to hear your familiar movements
  Lined up on the sheets that we lay in
  were the rocks I collected from the roads near our home

I heard my brother chanting alone
like a songbird with brightly spirits
  His love song so sadly unheard and rehearsed
  for the woman that strained his soul

What little time I had left here for you
and you were out of sight from my reach
  I dressed with your trousers held up by your belt
  meticulously placed each rock within

The ferocious beast in me soon to rest
Forlorn and broken at best
  Down the swamp with Angel's wings,
  Hail the thunder at last my soul sings

Worthy not to heaven's gate
lay me down on cold water slate
  Tempted hell on my lover's fate
  the love that found me came too late

Dedicated to Virginia Woolf

Forgiveness is the remission of sins. For it is by this that what has been lost, and was found, is saved from being lost again.

~ **Saint Augustine**

Perdono

~ The Pack

In my dreams, I shall not meet you
at the station by the spring
for when I wake it is all for nothing
that the mirror reflection is not mine

Years ago when I had you
I hurried away from your reach
now with beckoning voice you call me
yet this love affair can never be

For with tired hands you held out
Slowly, twice I died for thee
and for what was all this anguish
but in vain to not let us be

You who came upon me bathing
all temptress lust and lovely tales
me of heart and abandoned sounds
vowed this love would never fail

but in dreams was our only breath
and for this we have failed

in my dreams you shall not visit
to carry out what was not meant to be
I rest my life within your love
and ask you to forgive me.

~ Everyman

I, felt no objection to your strangest desires

I, but the mist in forms of your dreams

In dreams, you revealed your story to me

The nights of longing to be not to be

I was not desired by the hands that now bleed

Tulips sprang brilliance with colours of me

Dreamscape tore open the wounds,

I-scream-no-more

What could have been happy remained so sad

What was yesterday has grown sour and bad

Now empty and worthless as the mist forms anew

In dreams, I stood weeping for I had lost you

~ Sanctified Memories

you are gone
but not forgotten
in your space
remains my heart
lying naked on the cold floor
waiting patiently for you
to return to me
to start it again
a *sanctified* blurred in my mind
the vigorous way about you
in your fierce manner
you left me standing
naked and vulnerable
once sanctified and full of grace
now I am weak
from your anger
the only place I feel holy is on the floor
I don't know the reason why
I made you angry,
this time,
but you are gone,
in your space
remains my heart
lying naked on the damp floor
I wait
for you
to come again

memory

~ Spinning

as the world shifts to shadows

a watch, her wrist sets the time to

reveal

that

no forgiveness

prevents from hindering any shade

this woman, so full of ideas,

now

defeated

feeling her skin harden

without compassion to cling to

drowning as a delicate organ

sponging the bottomless souls around her

behind every flutter of her heartbeat

love dies

~ Cicatrice

Ho
preso
una
ferita
profonda
scuro
e
l'ho
portato
con
me
fino
morì

Il
perdono
perso
nel
tempo,
nello
spazio
della
morte,
in
questo,
la mia vita

~ Drowning

Binding my tail
soft scales overlapping
pry thee amidst my eyes

Surrounded in an irksome light
around the chute of the waterfall
seize me not from gushing
into fastened arms

If only for love,
spirits suffer in vain

You flutter around me
sinking your teeth right through me
See into me
If not for the outer layer
I would bring you my blood
in the holiest cup
knotted and refined
of Celtic spirit
and lurking faces

Spill on my arms
Outstretched and opened
Surge through my being
seek the hollow deliverance

now

Perdono me

~ My Castle Stalker

I know all your thoughts
listening to your breath as you sleep
counting the pain I feel, I remain awake
all the things you do not want from me
this is all implanted in my heart
but for love I must try
recalling all that was important to me
without any tones left
I must tell you now more than ever
that time is the only thing on my side
steadfast, I wish you near
no reasoning will come to me
I resist from speaking more and more
I find myself alone against your door
all the stupid things I have said
a lover's tongue scorned by no reply
words you do not understand
for a love that was not real

if in my heart you are the blood
the blood thins whenever you leave

in the silence beyond the stars
and the absence of your touch
I had but one wish
through my eyes you were my realization
but you never shared the same
and in my anguish, you remain my tears

last night he told me things I wanted to hear from you
I felt his **chest rip open** and the warmth of his heart
smother my being
how I longed for this
from you
and in the sombre of the night
behind the walls of your cast
I rushed to find you
once again, you, like a King, in her bliss
I wished for all this
from you
we enact and react to all that is never said
soon enough
you are well contented
feeling the softness of her flesh
her fingers sit longingly in your mouth
resisting nothing and taking her in
this is what I had wished
now I see the beauty that I do not possess
I see it in his face
he who draws near, you who moves away
denying myself to feel the bounty
of his love
desiring it only
in
you

Significant

The great art of life is sensation,
to feel that we exist, even in pain.

~ **Lord Byron**

~ The Womb

I recall
the night when my brother made way
for me around my mother's womb.

It was as if he had decided
he did not want to be in this world.
So he threw me closer towards
the placenta of her grief.

She stopped feeding me days later.
She sensed the deal my brother
cast with God and this made her
coarse with me.

I recall only one sound.
My right ear not being able
to hear anything
as my left ear had overextended itself.

It was my father crying from the other room.

Her endless abandoning stopped
the music from entering.
The more I talked,
the quieter I became.

~ My Italian Shoes

Father had three daughters.
Only two were born from the seeds of the old country

the other
the new country

The first was raised to be of angelic style,
follow life from the book,
go to Catholic mass,
ask for forgiveness.

The middle was raised to be the artist,
follow life thrashing the book about,
go around the world,
ask for mercy.

The last, he paid no mind to.
Followed life through seeking truth,
go from one task to another, alone,
ask for nothing
and create a circle of love
without him.

Speak to me now of love
and I will tell you I was no one's child

Mother had two daughters
who remained by her side.

~ In this garden state

In this garden state of hope
where the fiend reflects her childhood
Ada contemplates all that her mother should have been.
In her refuge of silence,
she waits patiently for absolute love.

This is the least she could have given to Ada.
All that she is, now, futile rejection and gutted loathe.
This, she will not force upon her womb.

A photograph of father holding her close to his chest,
whilst sisters' stand to either side of his strength.
She is wrapped,
firmly,
from the warm sun touching her face.
Tighter from his skin daring to touch this Love,
he will become her disease,
Yet, in the end, it will be she who will rise.

Creeping in low income with fears
of going blind and still waiting,
father comes to mind and Ada begins to cry.

He holds the synthetic cup fueled with a tank of booze
His hands are the hammers
that beat down mother's spirit.
She, the child that stands in the middle
to save them from each other.
Yet, now, as this child, she, alone, gets by.

~ The Front Porch

the front porch

Made of concrete cell-like
man filled prison echoes
built from father's thick hands
where he drank at night
every night

the front porch

Chairs from the kitchen table
wrapped in patterns of the old country
brown mixed with yellow and orange dead flowers
we were not the envy of the neighbours
only mocked by them

the front porch

The philosophical sofa
where stories unfolded about
father's sadness
and the red wine
tainted my thoughts
remnants of alcohol wet my hair

the front porch

Spelling textbook wide open
studying my words for the next day
while the tears from my father's eyes
dripped from pain onto the page
as I shouted out words in foreign tongues to please him

the front porch

Archways "times" four
brown brick distinguished the Italians
from the Protestants
mother was never seen sitting with us

the front porch

Around the corner from the garage
my father took the kitchen chair
walked with stride steps
determined
focused

the garage
the invisible tight-rope
the last conversation
hopeless

~ Joseph (Peppi)

My grandfather always wore the same trousers.
He was poor.
I was only a little girl.
I know he worked the field from dawn to dusk
and walked 8 miles to reach home.
The same suitcase style of woven donkey hairs
carried his meals three a day.
The shovel of steel made a groove alongside
his back where it lay during the journey home.
His hat was not fancy like the men in the shops.
It was of cheap cotton to keep the sweat off.
I remember him holding my hand in his
not understanding the stares of passersby.
The musk, the soil and the rain carried
themselves on his skin especially his arms.
He hated the sight of the potatoes in the marketplace.
Digging for them was his life.

I wonder now that he is gone
why his tapestry had been unkind.
He was a religious man, always seeking truth,
and so very shy.
From birth to death, I lived with him.
I longed to take his smile.
To place it on my son's faces to
show that love was worth the while.
His Vespa rests against the garage now and his
hat still hangs in its place.
His shovel is rusty, old and retired
but his memory is my carrying grace.

~ Ricordando

Energy
off the coast of remembrance
that one marked memory of time
when I was worth everything
I will tell you now my skin has chilled, dry, hard
the indicator of this deathly present life
what do you know about the European women?
what do you think you know?
I had so much faith in the father
more faith in the church and marriage
until I left home
here the Book of Laws slammed into my corridors
here where choices made
even though I convinced myself they were MINE!
mirrored the "more fool me"
robbed of the threshold gardens of a wondrous life
shocked from the rockets - minus - stars in the skies
my generation was not my mother's
although I tried
God. Damn(ed). You.
I tried
I am the identity of the deceased daughters
- none of them survived
and their voices
silent sleeping silent

~ Another man

unable to explain the grind and sperm between her teeth
she recaps false memories of last night lived
forming a vision of something horrible
where darkness is a part of the scenery
he does not buy it
the slammed door between her ears
he's gone

time now is all that stays with her
free falling through the empty room where he left her
the sound of agony crossing over the bed
her mind makes up why she cannot remember
fate spelling out letters on her bones
a naked figure

there is no story left to tell now
He does not come back to listen
She wants to believe it was the right decision
after all is life not already planned?

the choice of sleeping with another man

Lovers don't finally meet somewhere;
they're in each other all along
~ Rumi

~ Recalling Rosita

I remember when she was about 95

lived off the corner brick hut

in the southernmost part of Italy

about 15 miles from our home

on the mountain

sometimes she would get a ride

into the village to come see us

even, at 95

she always carried her crochet handbag

by her side

plump and still voluptuous

she had delicate lips

and seven daughters

she shouted when she cooked or prayed

made love-in silence

if you mentioned Thomas to her

her eyes arched forward

a black wave passed in front of her

~ Human Traffic

They place a tattoo upon your heart

not for us to see

black lines chasing white streets

leading to rooms, fermented and unknown

your father, your uncle, your brothers stared

hoping they would be the next one in

to see the damage never repaired

Your mother took the money

your sister paid the deeds

your aunties combed your hair

pretty Samina, if you please?

and all you ever wanted

was a bit of tenderness

Samina, holy prostitute,

boys and men, who knew you best

your tattoo spoke of swords

against your darkened skin

to pierce

into your chest it lies

Samina,

please don't die?

you waited in a room

spilling cum from the walls

praying for the lull within

a wooden narrow hall

a bed,

your body stretched and dissolved

spread her legs for lust
unwillingly every time
but did it in fear
for fear of the knives
she lay her head at night
looked over to the moon
no tears came easily to her
her destiny, her doom

she died

~ The price for a prize

They say the way to a woman's heart is flowers,

especially roses,

apparently I am supposed to get excited when

I see chocolate.

In fact, I am told that

chocolate and roses will "win me".

This makes me feel quite branded – like a cow.

Imagine his surprise when he sat next to me

on my porch that evening.

Children, gone, grown up now and left.

I find myself alone but it ain't painful

I can still read his mind, about me,

after all them years of begging to be free.

He came from around the back of my homestead

thought he was being clever

In one hand the roses, a smell of them

done gave me a headache

In the other, chocolate, I can't eat chocolate anymore.

Not that I ever did but nowadays with few teeth left

chocolate is not my first choice.

He is sweet, always had been sweet, but he isn't what wins

my heart.

that there be poetry

The deluge of fruitful diction, the bold nouns, verbs

and adjectives that take us beyond

our granite minds to similes.

that there be poetry

The silence as I sit in my room

the attachments of love, and loathing all on one page

that there is poetry

Where dreams are acceptable and you can be

whatever style, whatever size, whatever name

whatever relentless wish you want to be.

There is no prize for love with chocolate and roses
but there is a price for me
Words spoken
Words written
Poetry

~ Smeared Dress

Your offending eyes undressed me
your angry smile mistreated me
tonight was filled with regret
and I didn't even know you yet.

Up against the wall I slammed
you were going to be the man
that took my fortress within my tree
a wrath seethed inside of me.

Your hands were larger than my might
that bled upon the darkened night
your knees broke open my sacred grace
into my hole, my vessel place.

You filled it up with such disgrace
tonight I knew what was my place
smeared dress against the glass
selection of poison or grass
I chose the first to die quick
you forced the second
a massive stick.

Against my lips, I took it in
and gasped what was left within.
A smeared dress of Burberry scent
pit of hell, where I went.

Amour

Poetry heals the wounds inflicted by reason.

~Novalis

~ **O**n Being Ignored

Pampering words
when you need me
are never enough

You continue to represent
what you are not

I speak only in a true tongue
you are bad for my health

The abortion of us is not over
Thick syringe filled with toxic blood

Spews out from my mouth to your ears
longing in the form of

Being ignored

Act it out in the skull space of the mind
Apathy for your mourning fills my rhyme

The coma you are in is done via a mask,
injecting your silence like heroin destroys the task

~ My Personal Judas

I have never been loved
but I have been lied to

You are not alone
I know this
my mind tells me so

You are not alone
because the grove in which you walk
tracks dirty shoes now

And I saw your growth
pumping hard
on
her
camped out on your bed
having sex on top of you

Only
a few times
paradise has filled with flowers
between us

I picked them and
gave up my life for

you

thinking

maybe

someday

I would not feel so alone

Your hands swathe down her
and your eyes tell me
you enjoy her
too much
this grows my sorrow mused

cancer fills my stomach
a mucus spit waiting to fire
yellow-skinned bastard
sex does not last forever

moments pass in days
you gesture to me
you need me
there is
self assurance in loneliness
and bliss in fucking

her

without regard

~ **B**ad Blood

you were a long year
like wars between wars

I do not crave you, nor miss
what we had, *not*

the thin coat places itself on my skin
every morning

my arms raised against a wind
that is invisible to others

and I pray aloud to get His attention
He is there, never left, my own insecurities

I cry because I am sick of explaining
the truth

there is so much bad blood around me
I cannot write to make you feel better

this is not your life

~ Volare

Parasites filled in her belly
and the doctor suggests she stop smoking

she thinks it's the Greek salad from yesterdays bistro date
maybe she won't stay at the Stratford Hotel tonight
her body seems to shut down from the heat in the room
the snow outside dresses the weeds

she could have sworn she felt
several bed bugs on her neck

tomorrow is minutes away from waking

Maybe she'll call Roach in the morning
they could drive to the Ottawa Canal together,
that is,
if he isn't too busy

it's been a long year
she reserves no judgments
the order of things persist as
God's Will

the pillars of blood now turn
and the writing is never lost as they told her

Poverty, created without thought,
yet awareness throws blades and spreads light

~ Unwanted

Did you know you were unwanted

your philosophy of nothingness

always untrue

and as mysterious as a cat

Did you see the gift I gave you

or were the signs censored

recharging relationships

never did come that easy

Did you think I would be so foolish

To fall for your tragic story-again

That the woman in me

Would be beckoned by hopeless romance

Did you count those days with me

The days where you stole my thoughts

sorting them like trophies

collecting my vagina in your dusty box

Did you forget the faithlessness you drove

in one direction toward my eyes

how foolish, how foolish am I now?

Ask the elements to protect you,

oh no

love is so unkind

You and your magical wand

misleading me and my life

I was waiting for you

pacing for you to bring back my age

youthful love with hands up my shirt

but you went even higher and ate my words

Did you not notice the medal of courage

resting on my mantle near to your sword

you know the one you left under your pillow

surprise.

~ Parallel to you

Annie's veins run parallel
Insanity bathes in the lining of her bedroom walls
And she retreats to the shell where she is safe
yet to others she stands the Iron Maiden that never falls

It was just yesterday when Annie was proud,
of whom she was
If only she knew about all the mistakes,
she was to make
Her voice box now closed
She has killed herself several times today

Blinded and strangled by the dark dog demons
They never seem to sleep or rest
The dialogue that should be sweet
Drills a hole of loathing, making for a mess

Her mantra fastens her in constant form
For hope to ride and steal her away
No more hallucinations of grandeur
Denial keeps your voice astray

If you plan to grow your garden my friend
with patience and with time
Plant a seed that grows for Annie called
happiness without design

~ Insignificant

heavy steps
turning purple
cannot take the pressure
of my tiny soles
my rubber band mouth
heavy breasts
twisted nipples
inverted by the mouths
of babies suckling
my rubber band mouth stretches
heavy hands
tapping lightly
against the writing pads
of my rage
my rubber band mouth stretches to scream
heavy heart
tracing memories
about the life
spent
my rubber band mouth stretches to scream - sonno
now going cold
gone cold
tainted dreams now gone cold
delicate beings recklessly sold

i am the old woman i have been told
that sits unrested
and gone cold

~ Fatal Nights

Weave the wound and wrap the blood

sterile needles that puncture this love

gauge the gush spreading through your hand

pick up the wound for it falls like sand

seize the weapon you thrash on my chest

crawl before this rage-filled mess

carry the cup you shared with me

banishing desire that shall never be

damn the day I found you lonely

pity the fool I would become

taste my yearning that screams your name

and suck me dry with *muse* that shames

murder my will this hollow eve

stroke my wit and let me be!

~ Murder Me

Greed

that eats daily at my stomach

a deadly twisted form of apathy for you

spanking my intellect

caressing my moods

yearning for someone that is never true

speaks works of a damned poet

always transpires but never really exists

revulsion swims on the stream of disgust for you

like a spider caught in a black web

you form too many confusing questions in my mind

bitterness and hatred are what you feed it

gluttony so powerful

it could kill instantly on impact

I only hunger for the mortal truth

that love does not live here in this house

freaking, frantically waiting for

no reply from you

this is all you give to me

a tenderness of poison

corrosion of minds

the search is now ending

the spider is caught up in this web

that her only choice is understandable

she knows it all too well

yet this too has come too soon

strangulation

a very small neck

won't take a moment of your

precious time

~ **D**arker Side of love

You'll return being what you are
they stand around her
fence her in

the smell of manure lingers
throughout the fields of farmland
rain sent damp morning dew

they laugh as she shakes
from cold, from fear, from despair

the first one moves forward, slowly stuttering in his tracks
he is gruesome, fat slipping out of untidy trousers
smothering his lips on her
groping his way

punching and patting her down
like a boxer

she is knocked out from disgust

he bends, barely looking up

only momentarily

seeking the approval of his mates

the laughter, the chanting begins

he enters the virgin hole
bangs away at her so hard that

the others stand like trophies proud of his accomplishment
he rises, victorious

wipes his brow and throws his semen on her
she lies dormant as the next places his piece in her
on and on this goes

screams of violence within her mind tearing at the laces
she has used and reused to sew her soul

the last one
breaks the circle, he is angry and ignorant of the others

looking down at the virgin he is brought to tears
with one arm he lifts her and holds her close to his heart

can she hear the laughter around her
no one knows

~ Routines

Last night you came back
sturdy shoulders and swollen belly
from the night out with your mates

I hate when this happens but
it does twice a week
and all too well you are going to speak

There are times when I sit on the floor
hidden behind the front door of our house
and pray you do not return home

Maybe the fog will whisk you up
so I don't have to bear the burden of your
verbal plastic teeth shouting at me, again

How rushed my life is when you are away
remembering what makes you angry is exhausting
"don't leave the dishes in the sink"

My routine is ritual, habitual, compared to yours
the nights out consist of hanging your clothes
hoping Julie doesn't see the bruise from next door

There it is the dreaded key sound through the hole
"Where are you! Get down here this minute!"

I am, down here,
you kicked me again coming in,
someday, I hope you miss

~ Freya

The sun is spent

I have found in you a dying thing

You

to whom I beckon so near

I should prefer that you bestow upon me

your eternal love

You, in your art, express none to me

Life, vibrating likes the spirit of a lost love

is thus the dead thing

Words wronged the Goddess

lesser sun entered her light

withdrawn from the spirits that surround thee

you linger like the madman

drowned in the water of this vermin lust

a ruined, empty soul prefers to be cast out

burdened by a love so removed

and in the absence, the darkness,

repressed words

growth of blood slipping

enters my goblet

I feel you suffering thirst

~ Frigid Bones

Frigid mantling skin off my brittle bones

with dried palms and eyes wet from frost

my layers do not keep me warm

the heavy air brings the current home

entering with remoteness in my heart

wiping the ice columns from my brow

you sit pale eyed with your cup of tea

placing the screws into my feet

there is no shelter from the deafening light

and sun rests now on the other side

where the universe is greener with delight

and my green moon feels wrongs from right

colours of opium twisted through red

on the bed where I lay your gruesome head

from the gale twilight that storms our room

where you told me you wanted me much too soon

the hours were ours to keep in the night

while rain beckoned the earths flight

I carry my feelings through shades of grey

and watch from the window where you lay

the hours of dusk emerge as you open your eyes

bones fragile from your face hung portraits this night

and the scent of you I no longer desired

set flames in your soul of a cursed fire

Frigid feelings sit next to my hands

crippling my fingers taped to rubber bands

seizing my words that remain cold from your cries

it was for your diction that this worship has died

coating me gorgeous with treasures and wine

to succumb to an object of sexual twine

i yarn you up to set myself free

You gave me no console when you come inside me

~ Your wooden floor

Scratching at the bedpost

claws extended

I creep down with poise

abandoning your selfish erection

hoping you do not wake up

I am leaving you

with a massive spider web on your face

I hope you aren't too upset

I warned you

not to shout out my name

it will be harder to forget me now

No handshake when I finally

meet you at the gate

I know you will not be pleased

to see me, this time,

considering the mess I have left

around your eyes.

No uncomfortable embrace,

which means I do not have to wear a sweater

to avoid it

I detest your sour look

tired of you soaring through your body

wandering aimlessly in that one cell that

holds together your thoughts

I reach the ground

where your life sits

collecting dust and jagged hairs

shaved from days gone by.

I can hear your teeth grinding

your flesh moves in your bed

your greasy forehead drips with panic

turn over

please

~ Trapped

My tires slash your body when you cross.

I find you lying against the curve of the road

filled with debris and stones.

It is hard to get myself up, my knees tremble,

petrified, I move toward you.

Along the side of the car,

residues, remnants of your private parts.

The air filled with flesh and mortality.

I want to close my eyes and make you vanish.

That is not going to happen yet.

Head decapitated from your body.

Extensions of what you were lie to my left and my right.

Funny how I am not afraid of you this time.

All the moments of abashing are out of sight.

I, once, arranged myself next to you every night

praying that the tablets I had just taken

will dissolve quickly

before your hand reaches for me.

I do not want you anymore

deceiving myself that I did

because I was afraid to be alone.

Now

I am trapped in the crossfire

of your sins.

You were desperate to control my every inspiration,

nervous to please and appease,

to calm my movements.

Yet my words danced around your doubts

typing against your forehead;

that assaulting pressure.

I step closer to make sure I got you.

Forward with anticipation and relief, you are leaving me.

My movements curiously look down.

It is the only part of you I recognize.

Mangled beautifully
swimming in a velvet bath
rests your soul.

I got you

trapped before your hand reached my cunt

~ Old Photographs

The old photographs lie on the desk waiting to be filed,
like the memories stored in the vault of my mind.
They have rested in this place for years now,
accumulating over time like cobwebs.
Cobwebs that lead me from the desk
to the room we once shared together.
Together where you told me that I was every
new day and long luminous night.
Nights that swept past us as you embraced me
restlessly laying within our bed.
Bed of solitude gathers near the old photographs now,
like the dust forming against your specs.
Specs of visions that drive home what we once were,
myriad laughter and joy encircles your lips.
Lips melt watering turned to manic rage,
when I found you with her, the anger I had.
Had it not been for this,
the old photographs would have remained new.
New patterns of leaves form on my branches now,
of the misfit I have become.
Becoming whispers in conversation,
and a scorned face in old photographs of new.

~ Canopy

What pleasantries we have shared
underneath this magnificent canopy
filled with light
thoughts of liveliness and ease
as the stars flickered in the night
And to think I used to see the light of day
from this dark and fragile sky
and all I dreamed of was you,
sparkling with your elegant eyes
an empty canopy is all that is left
the day that our thoughts died.

It was December when you set it up
I prepared myself for the fall
yet sometimes it shocked with its warmth and
it surprised me with its calls.
At night, I would sit inside it
the closest link to you
and I would feel all around it
rough around the edges, yet so brand new
There were moments when I thought
it could never drop too low
and then it would shock me again
perhaps telling me there was no more warmth

In the spring, our canopy closed for good
and, yes, of course, I cried
but it told me that there was love between us
despite whatever died.

~ Crucified

when you smooth over your words,
in your eyes I still can see the fierceness of your loneliness
it's like marbles falling on a concrete
shattering the opening of who you are not,

its loud and bitter and your expressions are
of one being raped
they speak in a tongue so unordinary,
intense and dishonest
but this is what drives them to exist
and all their complicated lies
surround those delusions

I watch your face
I see you have crucified yourself
weeping eyes and a sombre stare
you are a survivor of the lust and hatred
but I still see the slash around your neck
that is something you cannot hide
but under the force that consumes you, you must turn green
like the leaves on the trees in springtime
you cannot escape this, this your truth, your beauty

you go home each night
the walls that surround your perfect space
are thick enough to warm your spirit
for the next day
and when you return they remain the same.

~ Surrender

on a night like this one

even when manic looks good

you rush my branches

chasing me with your bend-skinned eyes

and despite this disease I feel

the hunt is easy as I give in too quick

my roots start to show

what little water I have left to feed from

buds do not grow here with care

I see nothing but the layers of smoke

compressing my thoughts to stay

in a place of agony with *no surrender*

requirements to conform with guilt cards

that lay next to your contagious games

my strength is knowing what they say

the weakness of unfounded self esteem

the day urges me to rise

manic screaming towards the disgust

and drowning out the risk to win

injury and neglect dive in

a figure fat, low, stacked with paranoia

immobile and bond with need

the branches wilt and decent

a lump of coal

is left of me

~ Creed

From the voice of in my heart,
I release contempt for those
that devour false stories
and eat away at my fountain of truths
bending toward the devils sins
instinctually I surrender for peace.
The miserable winter creates excuses toward
an affirmation of blame, as,
unacknowledged mental anguish stay the same.
Shades live in dimness with crimson doom,
yet moans of isolation need now drape away.
I have tortured every single word they ached at you.
You deserve to desire a pendulum of love,
one that swings toward you.
Harbour none the misfortunes of this infancy.
Sangue
dried from the decades of wounds.
Swim away from this parasite of greed and
buy into nothing
for
this serpent
is it messenger of the devil's creed

~ Devil Tree

Dancing around the devil tree
surreal moments with you
love that failed from the start
grime caskets flowing around us
branches untouchable
SHOUTING
"love me as I am"
laughter was our music
the music died in delicate time
a pocketful of stars
move around the moon
like human locomotives
we twirled but never touched
arms extended
hands reaching for me
I wanted to hold you
diction denied this moment
grasping for each syllable
nothing else matters
you were a descendant of a dirty whore
I could not have leapt this low
never giving out and never giving in
our story, a tiny epic
we were both acutely aware
the devil tree rotting
pushing us farther apart
old tissue of bark slides again
lonely flesh creeps in

~ Mauro

Across the street
exactly next to the Roman Catholic Church
there lived Mauro
and his mama
in a chamomile life
sweet
He bade me a good day
every day
as he passed my door
toward work
My smile
bigger than his lips

Mauro loved me
tho, we never met bodies

There was one occasion only
when he stopped to bring me a gift

I cannot quite get this out of my mind
Red Shiny Shoes with heels from hell
Taller than him

An inscription under the soles spoke
puttana
and I could not help to think
'yes, please'

~ Confessions

I have confessions
within
of thoughts of us
that have died
the stories you created to keep me near
you are inside her tonight
you are no longer my worry
you fade away
From me
Tonight
I have a watchful eye
throughout,
of footsteps moving fast
away from mine
the inventions you created to keep me near
you have become my fear
I am no longer your pleasure
you fade away
Colourless
Black
Tonight
I had devotedly loved you
long before we met
but
you were sleeping
I embraced our destiny to keep you near
but
you have destroyed my sight
we are no longer lovers
you fade away
Fragile
Tonight

~ **U**nder this tree

The hush of distant crowds around
I am walking in my sleep
A feverish pain over my joints
The sound of crackling within
I was the woman who did it alone
and in this
ensued such suffering

why did you find me
under this nectar tree
now where my hands have gone cold
where my bosoms tighten if touched
i have become deaf when I hear you

oh love, speak oh love me
hillsides of mountain portions measuring my willing skies

speak oh handsome blood, speak oh of this sweet
tasting muse of love
and do not make those promises
to carry me
i no longer walk beneath your feet
speak oh handsome love
speak to me

Dedicated to William Blake

Sorrow

On the outskirts of every agony sits some observant
fellow who points.

~ **Virginia Woolf**

~ Ain't nobody's loss

Born in confusion
Living in fear
the terror of dejection
whenever you are near
can't process the data
when love is around
paranoid by the drama
fortunes not found
you never listen
to all that is said
so I go on wishing
that I was dead
imagine the world now
no depending on me
fearless and forgotten
how good can this be
dejection is not questioned
replacement at cost
and I am forgotten
it's nobody's loss

~ Homeward Bound

a complicated sadness
that suffers because of others
and the sofa it rests on
has a massive crease in the seat
I have tried to paint the walls
a sunflower to brighten those days
but colours are not where words lay
and in the bed that should be golden
upon the pillows of my dreams
the rushing water that scares my wake state
drowns me in my sleep
the voices coffer to my thoughts
that close more each day
the uninviting and horrid memories
of rejection never stray
this is my sadness
although it is something I want not to own
my throat has closed
and time is lost
and my anger fuels in droves
convince yourselves you know me
and rest assured in your souls
that I am just a tapestry
of muse that never grows

~ Poetry's final days

a funeral is set
for souls that are dead
for a spirit that is no longer home
and pyre that no longer roams

a casket is laid
gorgeous in its bed
for creatures to sleep
and spirits to reap

a longing no more
just earth in store
a mountain corrupt
of lava and mud
of venom and lust
of drink and of trust

a funeral takes place
no souls are in trace,
but one, the accused
for innocence
for muse

an angel stands clear
a victim of madness
entranced by his words
and visions of gladness

a goddess is scorned
for her art
bitter hearts torn
for her love
that was used
and her art
and her muse

the music is heard
the laughter is sought
the killer remains
dancing in his thoughts

the madness ensues
the anguish is gone
fingers tied to the bedpost
blood drips along

the wetness of her mouth
the moisture of her lips
the souls of the dead
you taught her this

her crime
her art
her passion
her words

~ Writer

You are non-conforming
and unconventional
God is a subject in white
sex is rubbish

metaphors are empty
the abstract thoughts
you don't write about
annoy the publishers

unmolested diction
poetry that is larger than life
you tick away, naked and
intoxicated
with an opened view
from your flat
to the tracks where
the insignificant
wander around the clock
open to nothing but empty wallets

you talk too much
because the faces that are
listening have since dead
mid sentence
but you write
because without it
you are nothing
and because of it
you are the worlds eyes

I picked up
a deep dark wound
and I carried it with me
until I died

For the past 25 years, there have been some brilliant followers of my work. For them,

The Dead

First published in 1998 in

Muse

~ Just the whore you wanted

Be damned
Be shamed

For nothing good are you.
You are nothing but pure and undying evil.

Be thrown and cast out, wither away, so that others may stomp on your ashes. Come, hungry tigers to feast on your flesh so that you feel pain for you know no pain like the one you created in me.

Be gone into the brightest light
for a brief glimpse at what you will never see again
fire!

Oh muse, muse, how my fingers
bleed on this doomed and dreadful fortress he built for me

bleeding so like a dam broken from the wrath
of the hollow soul that devours my veins and feasts at my liver

Death cometh soon on this infamous night
where betrayal and corruption feed at my ever
so corroded despair

Lead me, oh holy Jesus,
to the damnation of this lustrous life

Forsake me for I am mad, so trapped within the core of my shell and beaten with sunken words that I may feel all the horror I have done to he I so spoke words of love to. Take me beyond the crystal eyes that stare me blind in the night and cast me away oh sweet Lord. Fire me up! Let me burn in the shadows of hell. I am a traitor that breathes nothingness and nonsense into my lover's stomach. Blaming my madness is not what I will do now!

I blame nothing on no one but my condemned spirit
a soul that has become reckless in my consequence of life
Consoling the one I love now is no use to what I have done.
This is not my world any longer. I live my life through fear.

Let me suffer my storm.

Oh muse, sorrowful muse, nervous and straying, muse.

Drifting in the prison of my mind that manifests

all the infuriating thoughts that I have made.

Oh sweet heavenly Father take me now

if for nothing else to make me suffer, truly suffer, the heat, the coals I

placed under my lover's feet.

Abuse this naked being that stands before you.

Head hung low

Begging to be torn

to shreds by savage mutants in your keep

Pity me not brave being

swallow me now, pity me not and

move my soul away from me so that I may not have

this deadly life

I have followed Jennie Clarke and her muse for several decades: they live and breathe as one. She travels the universe of love, observing all. Love is not always wine and roses. Jennie uses all the colours in her palette to portray the many shades of love: light and dark, happiness and misery, desire and loathing.

Her words show us the beauty that is love, and the ugliness that it can become. Above all, Jennie shows us that love is a thing to be treasured and not taken for granted.

L.R. Munro

I was given this book by a friend and really was not expecting anything wonderful. I was wrong! This is brilliant stuff, the broad sense of language used creates such stark, blunt and sometimes tender, emotionally charged images you cannot fail to have your breath taken away. A roller coaster of work charged by the human spirit that encapsulates grief, pain, loss and love. More of a life lesson than an afternoon read.

G. Briar

There is little to be discussed with Sanctified Memories. If you do not get it, check yourself.

D. Porte

Jennie Clarke's legacy, a raw muse that drives the diction to the pen that beats against the paper. This is her second book of poetry. Her first book in 1998, *Muse: a collection of poetry* saw huge universal success.

She is a freelance writer, having published for newspapers, journals and anthologies. Jennie is currently working on *"Jackets of House Arrest"*, a series of short stories as well as an arrangement she is compiling with fellow writers and poets.

Photographers:

A special thank you to Helen Rutherford for your glorious friendship all these years and wonderful eye.

To Laurence Acland, for your unending talent.